THE BADLANDS:
Decadent Playground of Old Peking

Paul French was born in London, educated there and in Glasgow, and lived and worked in Shanghai for many years. His book *Midnight in Peking* was a *New York Times* Bestseller, a BBC Radio 4 book of the week, a Mystery Writers' of America Edgar award winner for Best Fact Crime and a Crime Writers' Association (UK) Dagger award for Non-fiction.

His most recent book *City of Devils: A Shanghai Noir* has received much praise with *The Economist* writing, '. . . in Mr French the city has its champion storyteller.'

Both *Midnight in Peking* and *City of Devils* are currently being developed for television.

paul@chinarhyming.com
midnightinpeking.com
chinarhyming.com

THE BADLANDS:
Decadent Playground of Old Peking

Paul French

VIKING
an imprint of
PENGUIN BOOKS

VIKING

Published by the Penguin Group
Penguin Group (Australia)
707 Collins Street, Melbourne, Victoria 3008, Australia
(a division of Pearson Australia Group Pty Ltd)
Penguin Group (USA) Inc.
375 Hudson Street, New York, New York 10014, USA
Penguin Group (Canada)
90 Eglinton Avenue East, Suite 700, Toronto, Canada M4P 2Y3
(a division of Pearson Penguin Canada Inc.)
Penguin Books Ltd
80 Strand, London WC2R 0RL, England
Penguin Ireland
25 St Stephen's Green, Dublin 2, Ireland
(a division of Penguin Books Ltd)
Penguin Books India Pvt Ltd
11 Community Centre, Panchsheel Park, New Delhi – 110 017, India
Penguin Group (NZ)
67 Apollo Drive, Rosedale, North Shore 0632, New Zealand
(a division of Pearson New Zealand Ltd)
Penguin Books (South Africa) (Pty) Ltd
24 Sturdee Avenue, Rosebank, Johannesburg 2196, South Africa
Penguin (Beijing) Ltd
7F, Tower B, Jiaming Center, 27 East Third Ring Road North, Chaoyang District, Beijing
100020, China.

Penguin Books Ltd, Registered Offices: 80 Strand, London WC2R 0RL, England

First published by Penguin Group (Australia) in association with Penguin Random
House North Asia, 2012

10 9 8 7 6 5 4 3 2

Text copyright © Paul French, 2012

The moral right of the author has been asserted

Cover and text design by Steffan Leyshon-Jones © Penguin Group (Australia)
Map and illustrations by Jason Pym
Printed and bound in China by RR Donnelley

CIP data for this book can be obtained from the National Library of Australia.

penguin.com.cn

'There are some secrets which do not permit themselves to be told . . . mysteries which will not suffer themselves to be revealed.'

Edgar Allan Poe,
The Man in the Crowd, 1840

'What swarmings of people in this world, an hour before its end!'

Joseph Roth, 1934

Hotel de la Paix

Dong'an Market

Ping-Movi Thea

DA YUAN FU HUTONG

The Camel Bell Furs & Curios

Grand Hotel de Pékin

MORRISON STREET

Police Station

Peking Union Medical College

HATAMEN STREET

CHANG'AN AVENUE　長安街

→ to Chienmen

Alcazar

Olympic Theatre

Roma Nightclub

S

→ to the Western Hills

哈德門街

Tung Tan Restaurant

→ to Paomachang Racecourse

LEGATION STREET　使館大街

→ to Legation Quarter

Hatamen Gate

→ to Peking Railway Station

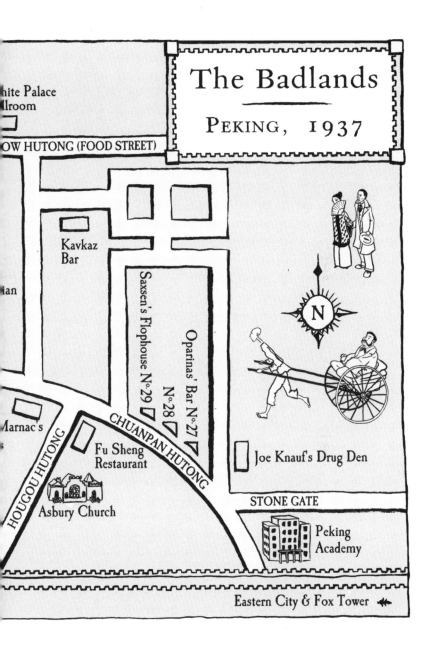

The Badlands

PEKING, 1937

White Palace
Ballroom

OW HUTONG (FOOD STREET)

Kavkaz
Bar

Saxsen's Flophouse No.29

Oparinas' Bar No.27

No.28

N

Marnac's

HOUGOU HUTONG

CHUANPAN HUTONG

Fu Sheng
Restaurant

Asbury Church

Joe Knauf's Drug Den

STONE GATE

Peking
Academy

Eastern City & Fox Tower

Contents

Introduction

he district of pre-communist Peking that came to be known as the Badlands flickered into life in the late 1920s, as a means of feeding the appetites of a certain sort of foreigner in the city. It was a place where the worlds of entertainment, prostitution, booze and dope came together with the yearning for sex, easy money and personal oblivion. A tight-knit warren of vice and lust and depravity, its period was brief, lasting only until 1941. Its heyday was the 1930s – Auden's 'low dishonest decade', a description that fitted perfectly.

The Badlands sat just inside the eastern flank of the Tartar Wall, which at that time enclosed the old Imperial City of Peking. Before the '20s the area was just a scrap of wasteland, used for little besides parading the bored foreign soldiers who guarded the embassies, which were known as legations in Peking, or for exercising horses. Once it took off as a nightlife destination it became a rookery of jerry-built alleyways, or hutongs. The properties were generally owned by Chinese speculators and rented to foreigners, who opened dancehalls, dive bars, brothels, cheap flophouses and restaurants. These foreigners were mainly stateless White Russians who'd fled the Bolshevik revolution, but Europeans and Americans were clustered in there too. The area was a multinational magnet for sin that came to life after dark.

In the 1920s, nearly three decades after the turmoil of the Boxer Rebellion and the siege of the legations, Peking's foreign community was feeling safer. A sense of complacency had set in, which was followed in the 1930s by a collapse in morality. Social mores spun off kilter, self-control and restraint broke down, and on the back of this the Badlands festered. The Chinese police largely chose not to interfere in the running of the place, leaving the foreigners to police themselves. As the Badlands grew, attracting the so-called foreign 'driftwood' of China, so any official control of the district spiralled downwards. Even the darkest desires could be fed there, catered for by the criminal and the corrupt, who felt themselves effectively untouchable within the confines of the rookery.

This world within a world was small compared to the areas that became known as badlands in other cities, notably Shanghai. It consisted of only a few narrow hutongs, with Chuanpan Hutong, running east to west, the main strip. The spot where Chuanpan met Hougou Hutong, running north to south, was considered the heart of the Badlands.

The northern boundary was formed by the traditional food street of Soochow Hutong, and the southern by the Tartar Wall, some eighteen metres high and twelve metres wide. The western border was Hatamen Street, across which lay the self-quarantined and exclusive Legation Quarter, with its embassies and European boulevards and respectable forms of entertainment. The calm serenity and polite society of the diplomatic compounds stood as the mirror opposite of the Badlands. Because the latter was small, everyone pretty much knew everyone else. So interconnected were they that their fortunes rose and fell along with that of those few narrow hutongs.

From September 1931 on, when the Japanese army invaded Manchuria, the Badlands' inhabitants and regular visitors were propelled by a sense that Peking's days were numbered. As Japanese troops moved south from occupied Manchuria and surrounded the city, the sense of doom increased. Peking's fortunes had been in a continual slide since 1911, when it was stripped of its status as an imperial city following the collapse of the Qing Dynasty and the creation of a republic. It had then been neutered politically in 1927 when Chiang Kai-shek moved the capital south to Nanking, leaving Peking effectively undefendable should Japan decide to pounce.

The Badlands had thus become a community of vice in the middle of a city slipping into chaos and turmoil. As Japanese aggression lurked beyond the city walls, Peking battled warlordism, communism and gangsterism, and was also afflicted by diseases of all sorts – smallpox, whooping cough, tuberculosis, periodic outbreaks of bubonic plague. The Badlands contributed one more, syphilis, and became itself an affliction on Peking, with its virus of uncontrolled lust, its venom of bad dope and tainted heroin. It was a symptom of Peking's slow and lingering decent from civilisation into barbarism in the interwar years.

In July 1937 Peking was finally invaded by the Japanese, but the Badlands survived to limp on through China's life-or-death struggle against the brutal occupation. By 1940, when the Second World War had broken out, the Badlands was inhabited largely by those who had to remain in China by necessity – White Russians who had no papers and so could not leave, criminals who were unable to return to wherever they had come from, the drug-addicted who could not risk being cut off from their suppliers.

Then came Japan's attack on Pearl Harbor, in December 1941, after which all Allied foreign nationals in Peking were interned in prison camps. The pace of the Badlands slowed further, but the brothels stayed open, opium and heroin continued to be dealt. With the defeat of Japan in 1945 the Badlands even briefly revived. It took the incredible convulsions of Mao's revolution in 1949 to finally sweep the old days away, following which the Badlands stayed forgotten for more than sixty years.

But what of the denizens of the place? Those White Russians, Americans and Europeans who had lived and worked there? It seemed as if they, along with the vices of the area, simply disappeared, leaving no trace whatsoever. And in the main they did leave no memoirs, no collected letters. There was very little in the way of a photographic record of their existence or their world, and the historical record consisted only of fragments, snippets and anecdotes of how these people came to be in China, in the ancient city of Peking, in those few narrow hutongs to the east of the Imperial City.

I first came to learn of the Badlands when I was writing *Midnight in Peking* (Penguin, 2011), an account of the ruthless murder of a young Englishwoman called Pamela Werner, daughter of the well-known British diplomat and Sinologist Edward Theodore Chalmers (E.T.C.) Werner. I'd had to search hard for the details that still existed, and since then the Badlands has continued to intrigue me, and, it transpired, many readers. People from around the world got in touch to pass on their recollections. Among them was the dancer Tatiana Korovina's daughter, then living in Australia, who contacted me with her mother's incredible story. Other members of China's old White Russian community, now scattered across the globe, also told me their memories, theories and tall tales.

While the Badlands might be forgotten in China, and unknown to today's foreign community there, it still lives on in the heads of these old men and women around the world. They just needed a nudge to tell their stories, reassurance that there was an audience who wanted to know about this world and its habitués. This extraordinary response inspired me to dig deeper still. It was evident that the residents of the Badlands – the outcasts of the supposedly respectable foreign community of Peking – were comprised of the good, the bad and the poor unfortunates. Their lives, it seemed to me, deserved to be recorded. Hence this slender volume.

Slender because official details remain hard to capture, and when they do exist are only brief. A note in a police file here, an embassy record there, and then the person slips away again into anonymity, like a radio station that can't quite keep the signal and whose voices are lost in the static. The winners, they say, write history, and by and large the people of the Badlands were losers – the exploited, the addicted, those hiding from past lives and failures or running away. Most could never, or would never, tell their stories out of guilt or shame. Others believed their stories to be worthless.

Some of the inhabitants of that lost place appear to have had no redeeming features at all. The American Joe Knauf dealt violence and fear as well as drugs, the pimp Saxsen had no regard for the women he exploited. While both men left little trace, the chilling nihilism of their lives comes across clearly in the accounts of them by contemporaries.

The legacy of others is more problematic. Were two of the best-known White Russian madams in Peking, Brana Shazker and Rosie Gerbert, irredeemably awful? Those who still remember them saw both sides of these women: they were profiteers from prostitution, to be sure, but they had started out as victims of it. Then there were the White Russian prostitutes Marie and Peggy, whose working lives were truly dreadful, and who bonded together until the harshness of their situation drove them into separate pits of madness and addiction.

Through these two women we can glimpse the daily life of the Badlands. We know that, for a short period at least, they appeared carefree and happy. They window-shopped in the department stores of Morrison Street and the Legation Quarter, visited the bakeries, delicatessens and cafés run by foreigners in the city, and surely found some time, before life became too hard, to visit the nearby Ping-an cinema to see the latest movie from Hollywood.

For all that it was a drawcard for the sinful and the decadent, the Badlands was also a place where people strove to carve out decent lives for themselves, to fall in love, marry, raise families, and build successful careers in the entertainment industry. Tatiana Korovina's is one such story. A White Russian girl who knew the thoroughfares of the district intimately, she did not succumb to their vice but instead fell in love, married, had a family, and eventually left China to lead a long and happy life.

Even as terrible things happened – suicides, murders, war and internment – the hustle and bustle of everyday life went on. Night-soil coolies passed through the alleyways in the early mornings, the smells of local delicacies and street food wafted down from Soochow Hutong, while the clang of the trolleybuses and the rhythm of the rickshaw pullers' feet slapping the roadways formed the soundtrack. One former habitué recalls standing in the epicentre of the Badlands – at the junction of Chuanpan and Hougou hutongs, where prostitutes, beggars, drug dealers, pimps and nightclub touts all gathered to wait for punters – and looking up to see the stars in the Peking sky. There were moments of calm and beauty even among the chaos and filth.

Those few years when the Badlands sprang into life after dark and died down again when the sun came up can seem illusory, and hard to grasp. It is perhaps fitting, then, that the man generally acknowledged as the King of the Badlands was such an enigma – a being of indeterminate sex known generally as 'Shura'. He is remembered by some as little more than a vagabond Russian with a charming smile and a way with an anecdote, while others recall an extremely clever master criminal who amassed a fortune, through having a hand in every Badlands operation that was going, from owning the cabarets, girls and drugs to overseeing bank robberies. The truth, it seems, lies somewhere in between: the Badlands was an area that gave rise as much to exaggeration as to excess.

Some of the old hutongs that made up the Badlands still exist, sandwiched between modern Beijing's main roads, which are plagued by traffic congestion. There are hutongs that date back to before the fourteenth century, but Chuanpan and Hougou hutongs are no older than the 1920s. At first glance they appear typical, but look closely and you'll see a distinctly 1920s/'30s feel to the architecture and the stonework. Several buildings might just qualify as art deco or modernist, the Chinese builders having adapted Western styles and flourishes.

Chuanpan (now Chuanban) and Hougou hutongs bear little resemblance to their former selves, and their current inhabitants have no idea of the louche past of their neighbourhood. Today it's mostly home to families of migrants from China's hinterland, come to find their fortune in the capital. Small budget hotels cater for visitors from the provinces; there are kiosks selling mobile phones to aspiring businessmen, a printer who can produce name cards for you in a matter of minutes, barber shops, tobacconists, cheap restaurants selling regional specialities so the new migrants never feel any culinary homesickness. On Chuanban Hutong, opposite the Oparinas' old bar, Brana Shazker's brothel and Saxsen the pimp's flophouse, now stands a modern school with a large playground. It's a friendly community, crowded but seemingly happy, endlessly optimistic in the way modern China excels at.

Apart from the odd architectural flourishes, there are a few things that show the history and continuity of the area. The Asbury Church – the 'Island of Hope' – still exists, and is open for business just as it was throughout the heyday of the Badlands. And the northern boundary of the old rookery, Soochow Hutong, is still a busy and crowded food street, selling *jianbing*, deep-fried *youtiao*, spicy noodles – pretty much the same fare as was bought by the old denizens of the Badlands, hungry after a night's entertainment or work.

But the day will come when even those few remnants will disappear. As will those people who lived through the decade in which the Badlands thrived, or the one during which it survived occupation and war. I hope that the following stories will bring some of the old Badlands of Peking back to life, in both its positive and negative aspects, before the memories of the world that existed within those few narrow hutongs are gone forever.

The Dancer
How Tatiana Korovina
Became Lilian

 n the late 1930s it was not uncommon for the landlords of Badlands flophouses to discover a short-term tenant dead in their room, having taken an overdose the night before. Whether accidentally or on purpose it was never clear, but either way, the landlords learnt to frisk the pockets of their tenant for the day's rent before calling an ambulance. In the winter months the owners of brothels and bars might open their doors to find the frozen, lifeless body of one or other of the Badlands' old Russian beggars – aged Tsarist officers with no saleable skills left, or old widows too haggard now for prostitution.

Suicides were commonplace, the penniless giving up the fight against poverty, those who had fallen into prostitution finally deciding that death was preferable to the miserable life they were living. And every so often tempers flared, courtesy of cheap spirits, especially the rot-gut *samogon* – illegally distilled vodka that was cooked up in backyards. Then scores would be settled, and a man might die with a knife in his gut or a bullet in his head. Many who ended up in the Badlands never left; it was the final stop on a downward spiral.

Still, new life also entered the district. The Asbury Church on Hougou Hutong, home to the China Inland Mission, was run by well-meaning American Methodist missionaries, who every week would find an unwanted white baby or three left on the doorstep during the night. Notes in Russian were pinned to them, begging mercy and forgiveness for these infants whom the mothers themselves could not support. The missionaries took the babies in and tried their best, which was why the Asbury came to be known as the Island of Hope.

The Badlands *was* bad. It was cruel, and life was truly cheap there. But for some it was also exciting, and there was a community, of sorts. One person who thought of it as home was Tatiana Korovina, a pretty White Russian girl born in Shanghai in 1919. Her parents had managed to make a life for themselves in China after fleeing the Bolsheviks in 1917; her maternal grandfather had been a delegate at the Tsarist Prince Kudachev's Russian Legation in Peking, and was stranded there after the Russian Revolution.

Tatiana, known to her family as Tania, got a decent enough education, and she also loved music. Trips with her parents to hear the largely White Russian Shanghai Philharmonic at the Town Hall on Nanking Road were a special treat. In 1922 the Russian ballerina Anna Pavlova visited Shanghai on her first Oriental tour, dancing *The Dying Swan*, and Tatiana's mother was swept up in ballet fever, along with many others in the city. She sent her daughter to dancing classes with the Russian émigré teacher George Goncharov, who had danced with the Bolshoi in Moscow before the Bolsheviks came. One of Tatiana's fellow students and friends was a girl called Margaret Hookham, whom everyone called Peggy.

Ballet flourished in Shanghai, and the two girls were taken to see California's famous Denishawn Dance School troupe, which visited with a special Orientalist repertoire. They also saw touring modern dancers such as Irma Duncan, a protégé and adopted daughter of the great Isadora Duncan. Peggy Hookham, whose Irish father worked for British American Tobacco and whose Brazilian mother was hopelessly glamorous, was subsequently sent as a teenager to ballet school in England, while Tatiana's family moved to Peking.

Peggy went on to study under Ninette de Valois in London. She joined the corps of the Royal Ballet, then based at Sadler's Wells, and changed her name to Margot Fonteyn. Tatiana Korovina continued to practise dancing whenever she could in Peking; she joined the chorus line of a local dance troupe that played the venues of the Badlands, and changed her name to Lilian.

The Shura Giraldi Troupe was small, half a dozen girls at most and a Russian gypsy guitarist, but it was the best known of the few dance ensembles in Peking. It couldn't not be, given that its patron was the notorious White Russian hermaphrodite Shura Giraldi, the uncrowned King of the Badlands, with a finger in every pie, so it was said (or rather, whispered). The troupe performed regularly at the best clubs on the edge of the Badlands, in what the Chinese referred to as the North Settlement Area – at the White Palace Ballroom, Marnac's French-style joint, and at the Alcazar, the Olympic Theatre, and the Roma Nightclub. The latter three were all next door to each other at numbers 3, 5 and 9 Chang'an Avenue. Awash with neon signage, like a mini version of Broadway's Great White Way, the avenue was close to the smart department stores, cinemas and hotels of Morrison Street. Shura's troupe also danced at the Manhattan Nightclub in the Badlands proper, a favourite of US Marines stationed in Peking, who demanded the latest Hollywood and Broadway hits.

Private parties added to the troupe's workload. Rich Chinese who liked to dine with gold or silver chopsticks and bowls at their banquets wanted foreign dancers to entertain their friends and business associates. The Japanese, who Shura knew all too well, would rent the White Palace Ballroom complete with Shura's troupe of scantily clad white girls on stage, for the amusement of those Chinese willing to collaborate with them.

The girls in Shura's troupe had heart and stamina. They were professionals, all having trained at White Russian ballet schools, they were quick learners, and they could keep a smile permanently on their faces, no matter how sore their feet. They didn't just perform in Peking, but went on tour. In Shanghai they danced on a bill with the Paramount Peaches, the city's best-known foreign dance troupe, made famous by their choreographer Joe Farren. Also an exhibition dancer and a gambling-joint proprietor, Farren was something of a Far East version of George Raft, having come from Vienna's Jewish ghetto to Shanghai to make his fortune.

In a few years Farren would fall foul of the city's more ruthless gangsters, and of the Japanese, but in the late 1930s he ruled the Shanghai nightlife roost. The nightclubs in the International Settlement and Frenchtown where Farren organised the entertainment – Ciro's, the Paramount, the Canidrome Ballroom – were legendary, dazzling venues that put Peking's much smaller establishments to shame. Farren's shows always boasted the classiest routines and the most gorgeous girls in the swankiest costumes.

The costumes worn by Shura's girls, and the routines they performed, were largely copied from the Broadway Melody movies, or from anything by the mighty Ziegfeld and his Follies. Tatiana slayed the crowds with her Marlene Dietrich outfit and routine, adopting a lilting voice in Songspiel style, and a drooping, half-smoked cigarette. Peking had never seen such Mitteleuropa class, sophistication and all-out sexiness before.

The other tour stops were mostly to the north of Peking, in Manchuria and in the strongholds of China's Russian-exile community:

the treaty port of Tientsin; chilly, industrial Mukden, up towards the border with Japanese-controlled Korea; and Harbin, close to the border with the Soviet Union and home to one of China's largest White Russian audiences. In the 1930s Russian-style entertainment was all the rage – gypsy jazz, the balalaika, mournful ballads of exile from the motherland mixed with the latest songs from Broadway and dance routines from Hollywood. There was a multinational audience of foreigners and Westernised Asians across the continent who yearned for these cultural forms, and so the troupe travelled further afield as well, to Tokyo, Yokohama, Manila and Penang.

It was a vagabond life of costume trunks and lodging houses with lumpy mattresses. Each leg of the beds had to be immersed in a tin of kerosene to discourage fleas. Greasepaint was applied in cramped backstage rooms; new dance sequences were learnt on the decks of packet steamers from Amoy to Port Swettenham. In remote Chinese ports like Weihaiwei, Chefoo and Port Arthur, the Shura Giraldi Troupe was the most stylish act ever to come to town.

Life on the road did have its good side. The girls enjoyed late nights in Singapore cabarets where wealthy white men with suave European accents smoked opium-tipped cigarettes, and they were showered with money from the audience in Yokohama. On the down side, they weathered propositions from lonely Dutch coffee farmers in Batavia, and clumsy gropes from sexually frustrated British rubber planters in Kuala Lumpur. But back in their heartland of eastern Peking they would eat late-morning breakfasts with adoring male fans who declared undying love for them.

When Tatiana, at just sixteen, was accepted into the troupe, it was after an audition by Shura Giraldi himself, and it was he who dubbed her Lilian. When she first met Shura he was a slight man with famously petite feet and a perfect set of small white teeth. He was always immaculately groomed and dressed, and wore his hair slicked down. He supervised the troupe but left the rehearsals and choreography to another White Russian man, who before the revolution had run several well-known *Cabarets Russes* at home.

Tatiana remembered Shura as a kind man who treated the girls with respect and kept his hands to himself, something that was rare among the men who ran the Badlands. Shura owned a house near Paomachang, in the Western Hills, out by the racecourse where foreigners loved to raise and race their stout Mongolian ponies and the Chinese loved to bet on them. While visiting the house with the other girls, on a short break from the city and its political tensions, Tatiana looked up from doing her nails to see an impossibly gorgeous woman in a long dress coming down the staircase. It was Shura, dressed for a date with 'some big shot', as Tatiana described it to her young daughter, years later and far away from the Peking Badlands.

This was the first Tatiana knew of Shura's famous hermaphrodite sexuality. The other girls in the troupe, better versed in the ways of the Badlands, teased her for her naivety – Shura was a he/she, whose company was much sought after by rich foreign businessmen and Chinese warlords. After that visit to the Western Hills, Tatiana became used to seeing Shura in his flowing purple dressing gown, gossiping with the troupe members and sipping syrupy liqueurs that stung your teeth they were so sweet.

One of the regular haunts for the Shura Giraldi Troupe, the Roma Nightclub, was owned by a well-known Italian doctor in Peking, Ugo Capuzzo. Just outside the Badlands proper, the Roma was almost respectable, almost elegant. It showed movies too, sometimes, and Tatiana always liked performing to its more upmarket and sophisticated audience. She also decided she liked the manager, Roy Tchoo, a half-Chinese, half-English man just a couple of years older than herself, who was making his way in the business world of the Badlands.

Roy came from good Chinese stock on his father's side; his grandfather had been a high official in the Foreign Service of the Qing Dynasty, the Tsungli Yamen, while his great-aunt was the stylish and independently minded Tchoo Ch'i-hui who married Hsiung Hsi-ling, China's Minister of Finance (and briefly Premier) under Yuan Shih-kai. The latter, 'China's Machiavelli', had boldly declared himself Emperor in 1915, then died of kidney failure less than a year later at just fifty-six. Roy's nationalistically inclined father had studied at Oxford, where he met an Englishwoman who was not easily put off by the social mores of the time, which frowned on mixed-race relationships. They married; Roy was born in London and the family left England for Japan, to join Dr Sun Yat-sen's Tongmenghui, or United League, in support of a republican uprising in China.

Roy held a British passport and was generally considered a good-looking and charming man. Due to his influential position and his family background, he perhaps suffered less prejudice than other Eurasians did, but then pedigree and ethnicity were less important in the Badlands than in other parts of foreign Peking, where snobbery and exclusivity reigned. Either way, Tatiana fell in love and married him, at just eighteen. Roy was stylish, cool; he and Tatiana would cruise the streets of the Badlands on his motorbike, Tatiana clinging closely to him as they threw up a dust trail behind them. They criss-crossed Peking on that bike, up to the Western Hills, out to the Paomachang Racecourse, attracting looks all the way.

A year later, in 1938, they had a daughter, Sylvia, who went on to attend the Convent of the Sacred Heart School on San Tiao

Hutong. Run by the Franciscan Missionaries of Mary, the convent also contained an orphanage, and it was from here that some two decades earlier the British diplomat E.T.C. Werner and his wife Gladys Nina had adopted an abandoned White Russian baby girl they decided to call Pamela. The Werners lived adjacent to the privileged enclave of the Legation Quarter, which was just the other side of the ancient Tartar Wall from the Badlands but light years away in every other sense. Pamela, intelligent, troubled, fun-loving, was just nineteen years old when she was found brutally murdered by that same wall, one freezing January night in 1937.

Tatiana and Roy saw the Badlands through to the bitter end. Though they lived and profited from its entertainment economy, they lived alongside danger too. When Sylvia was older, her mother warned her to stay away from certain men in the area, men who Tatiana knew were trouble. She and Roy moved on the periphery of their perverted world; they saw the excesses that could be indulged in across the lightly policed Badlands, and they were under no illusion that the place harboured some truly evil and disturbed people. By 1939 Roy was being pressured to screen Japanese propaganda movies at the Roma. He refused, on the grounds that he was a British subject, and that night the Roma burned to the ground. The arsonist was never captured, the Japanese police expending little energy in their search.

After the attack on Pearl Harbor, Tatiana, Roy and Sylvia were sent to Shantung province, some three hundred kilometres to the south. There they were placed in a Japanese internment camp for Allied nationals, the innocuous-sounding Weihsien Civilian Assembly Centre, along with so many other Peking residents, from both ends of the social spectrum. Bankers and diplomats of the Legation Quarter lined up with prostitutes, pimps and thieves from the Badlands to march into the camp.

Many of the more respectable foreigners were shocked to see what had become of those compatriots who'd got lost in the Badlands. One 'captive of a dope addiction', rousted by the Japanese from a Badlands den and transported to Weihsien, was described as 'wan, a paper thin ghost of a man, with dirty, torn clothes, scraggly beard and sea green complexion'. These people were the 'driftwood' of the Badlands, who until now had rarely surfaced, who never ventured north of Soochow Hutong, west of Hatamen Street or south of the Tartar Wall – the Badlands had become their entire world.

Internment was a harrowing experience even before the Tchoos reached Shantung. While they were being herded to the Peking Railway Station at Chienmen, a man darted out of the watching crowd of Chinese and grabbed the valise Tatiana was carrying. Inside were most of the family's photographs and jewellery as well as marriage and birth certificates, but the Japanese prevented Roy from pursuing the thief.

Staying strong together, the family managed to survive the camp until their eventual liberation by American troops in 1945, after which Tatiana, Roy and Sylvia returned to eastern Peking to pick up the pieces of their life. They found the Badlands a shadow of its former self. Roy took over both the Olympic Theatre, next door to the old Roma on Chang'an Avenue, and the Manhattan Nightclub, which attracted the US Marines in Peking as well as the Flying Tigers – American fighter pilots who had flown for the Chinese air force during the war. He made extra money by distributing movies in northern China, Manchuria and Inner Mongolia for the J. Arthur Rank studio.

But the Badlands' days were numbered. After the communist revolution in 1949 the Tchoos were effectively placed under house arrest in Peking for four years. Eventually, in 1954, they escaped to Hong Kong. Other family members were less lucky. One of Roy's brothers, John, was jailed during the Cultural Revolution and finally died in Peking. All of John's memorabilia of the old days, and his photographs of Tatiana, Roy and the Badlands, were thrown out into the front yard and burned by the Red Guards.

Roy and Tatiana, with young Sylvia in tow, moved on from Hong Kong, which was only a temporary stop for most of the European refugees fleeing China. They took ship and headed to Australia, the destination of many of their compatriots. Communities of White Russians grew up in Sydney, Melbourne, Brisbane, and still exist there. Tatiana and her family settled in Melbourne.

After the teeming concrete jungle of Hong Kong, the maddening incestuousness of Weihsien, the crowded backstreets of the Badlands, and, before that, Shanghai, Asia's largest city at the time Tatiana was born there, the space and fresh air of Australia came as a massive relief. Tatiana loved the climate, Roy the freedom, and Sylvia at last had a stable environment in which to grow up, untouched by war, revolution or the vicissitudes of Badlands life.

*Tatiana does
Shirley Temple*

*Tatiana's sailor
suit costume*

*Tatiana vamps up as
a smoking Dietrich*

*Tatiana among the
cherry blossom*

*Tatiana & Roy celebrate
a Peking Christmas*

*Tatiana in the Badlands on
Roy's motorbike*

The Madams
Brana and Rosie
Come to Town

rana Shazker and Rosie Gerbert had known each other since they first arrived in China. They had a shared history, a terrible one. Both were Russian-Polish girls from Bessarabia, a region now split between Moldova and the Ukraine; both had been lured by good-looking men in their home towns and taken to London, where they were broken in by being repeatedly raped in a filthy lodging house near Waterloo Station.

They were then set to work in East End brothels, and having learned their trade were shipped out to the East, following the trade routes of the Empire. Theirs was not an unusual story for poor Eastern European girls in the last days of the nineteenth century – they were part of the infamous white slave trade.

There were more bad times to endure in the new century. The First World War and the collapse of the old Russia brought floods of White exiles to China, with little more than the clothes on their backs. By the early 1920s Russian prostitutes were so plentiful in Peking, Tientsin and Shanghai that Brana and Rosie had to charge less than a dollar per customer.

Young trafficked quarry they might have been, but they rose up through the ranks. They mastered the business and reached a point where they controlled their own houses, Brana in big, bustling, cosmopolitan Tientsin in northern China, and Rosie in the small treaty port of Newchwang, on the Gulf of Pechili in Manchuria. It was said of Brana that she had brains; she knew how to keep her punters happy and the police and politicians on side. Prominent Tientsiners were never charged at her brothel on Bruce Road, in the British Concession, and so everything remained smooth.

Brana's only competition were the Polish-born Jewish Sanger sisters, who'd come to China early and been in business since the Russo-Japanese War of 1905. The sisters were known to have put their own daughters to work in their brothel, alongside trafficked French and Belgian girls, and with the Sanger husbands providing the muscle, it was altogether a family business. The Sangers kept another joint, which specialised in servicing Russian sailors, in Japanese-controlled Port Arthur, just across the entrance to the Gulf of Pechili from Tientsin. They had a third sister back in Europe who procured girls for their operations, and sent them on to Tientsin with the help of the French *soutenur* gangs, smuggling them out through Marseilles.

The Sanger brothels were generally regarded as filthy, low-class pits of syphilis best left to sailors. Brana wasn't interested in running that kind of place, and while hers weren't much better she did have some standards. Any girl of Brana's who got hooked on dope, took a little too much liking to the booze, got herself poxed, or ripped off punters (without prior permission) was out, no questions asked. Out of Bruce Road and, thanks to Brana's good relations with the local law enforcement, out of the treaty port and on a train to wherever, with no possibility of return. Cross Brana Shazker and you were dead in Tientsin. Now she was looking to expand by opening up in Peking.

The problem for Brana was that Peking wasn't anything like Tientsin. Tientsin was a treaty port; the police there were Europeans, as were the local politicians, and with a bit of compromise they could all get along. The Chinese in Tientsin were fine too. Brana did plenty of business with them, especially the few remaining Northern Warlords who liked to check her place out sometimes, procure some white flesh for a change. But she hadn't seen much of the warlords lately; they'd either been killed, grasped which way the wind was blowing and become 'patriots', or retired. Her clients still included a group of the old Russians, mercenaries who'd fought with the warlords up and down Manchuria, but by 1937 they too were getting old and tired or had died.

The Badlands, on the other hand, was policed by the Chinese, and loosely policed at that. There'd been trouble in the brothels there. After a particularly bad incident in one of them, a place on Chuanpan Hutong run by former US Marine Michael Consiglio and his 'wife', Madam Leschinsky, the pair decided they'd had enough. Besides, everyone knew it was only a matter of time before the Japanese took Peking, and to survive you'd need to deal with them. Consiglio, who still had contacts in the Marines in Tientsin, had heard that Brana Shazker was looking to set up in Peking. Wanting a quick sale, he offered her a knockdown price.

Brana had always dealt with the Japanese in Tientsin, those who had a taste for white girls, and she found them straight enough as customers, though inflexible when it came to money. Brana knew she'd eventually have to deal with the Japanese in Peking too, even in the Badlands, but Consiglio's price was too good to refuse. She took on the lease in Chuanpan Hutong in 1937.

Whatever anyone else thought of her, Brana saw herself as having a bit of class – a madam of the old school, more a sophisticated bordello lady than the foul-mouthed boss of a whorehouse. She knew she needed someone with a bit more bite to manage a place in the rough environs of the Badlands. That's when she remembered her old friend Rosie Gerbert, up in Newchwang. Serendipity all round: Brana needed a madam with enforcement skills to run the place, Rosie Gerbert – in Brana's experience always reliable in such matters – needed to get out of Newchwang and was in search of a job.

The deal was perfect. Brana Shazker had got the premises and the staff for a song, and Rosie moved herself down to Peking to sort out the day-to-day affairs. Brana installed herself in the best suite at the Hotel de la Paix, a Western-style building situated in a smart location on the upscale hutong of Da Yuan Fu, just off Morrison Street and a stone's throw from the Legation Quarter. The hotel had originally been known as the Telegraph Hotel, home to the engineers of the Great Northern Telegraph Company, which established the first system that connected Peking to the outside world.

Brana travelled back and forth between Chuanpan Hutong and Bruce Road on the first-class-only train – the so-called 'International'. She let her loyal Tientsin punters know that Brana's now had a branch in Peking – like Kiessling's ice-cream parlour on Tientsin's Racecourse Road, which had branches all over, or Whiteway & Laidlaw, with department stores in Shanghai, Calcutta and Hong Kong. Brana Shazker's brothels in Tientsin and Peking had beautiful clean girls guaranteed (just don't look too closely).

Two places meant double the revenue, and less financial risk in the event of one getting shut down. Moreover Brana could shuttle the girls back and forth between the two, so that the punters always thought there was fresh talent in town. Now Brana had a string of houses, just like her Tientsin rivals the Sanger Sisters. A sweet deal indeed.

Except that Rosie was something of a loose cannon. There was a good reason she'd wanted to get out of Newchwang, and fast. One of her girls had wound up dead and her body had been found near Madam Rosie's house. It so happened that the girl was known to have been saving to get out of the business, and she'd had about eight thousand silver dollars' worth of jewellery and seven thousand dollars in cash. When the police raided Rosie's house they found the missing cash and jewellery in her sideboard.

Rosie didn't seem too surprised at the stuff being there – she was just looking after it for her girl, she claimed. But only the most naïve citizens of Newchwang believed Rosie was not mixed up in some way in the business and it took a reputedly massive bribe for the police to forget about it. They still insisted she get out of Newchwang within twenty-four hours and never come back. She was now broke and had nowhere to live. So it was back to being a manageress of a brothel, the only business she knew. Brana Shazker's offer of a job in the Peking Badlands was perfect.

The big drawback with Rosie was her fearsome temper, which she lost pretty regularly and often spectacularly. She had Russian blood but had been born in Poland, though that border was a moveable feast. Having no passport she was officially a stateless White Russian émigré. Sometimes she claimed to be purely Polish, sometimes Russian, whatever suited her mood, which was pretty much always foul. She could famously launch into a tirade that would make a sailor blush in half a dozen languages.

At the time there was a circuit of brothels in China that were stocked with white girls and catered to white males. The circuit had been in place since the late nineteenth century and included all the treaty ports and towns where foreign navies put in across China, as well as Hong Kong (in the establishments along Lyndhurst Terrace), and points as distant as Yokohama (the legendary Nectarine), Singapore (Madame V's), Saigon (the famous Rue Catinat), and Manila. The madams and the pimps moved girls around to keep the customers interested, and the girls, for their part, gossiped and swapped contacts, tips and recommendations.

There were good destinations and bad destinations. 'The Line', Shanghai's infamous strip of bordellos along Kiangse Road in the International Settlement, was controlled by the most famous of all the China-coast madams, Gracie Gale, a legend in the business. Her 'resort' at number 52 Kiangse Road was the model for high-end joints in China. But Shanghai also had a district known as the 'Trenches', in Hongkew, notorious for being where many trafficked girls ended up, along with prostitutes who were at the end of their line – old, scarred, drugged, diseased.

Other brothels catered specifically for sailors. Before setting up in Newchwang, Rosie had worked at the Whisker's Girl House in the port of Weihaiwei, the northern base for the British Royal Navy, while across in Russian-controlled Port Arthur was the rather cheekily named American Legation Brothel. Before Brana became the queen of Tientsin's brothel business, it was run by the notorious casino and brothel manager Tientsin Brown. He had reigned from the early 1900s until after the First World War, expanding out of Tientsin to Shanghai and smaller treaty ports, building up a gambling as well as a brothel empire. Brana sought to emulate Brown, at least in respect of the brothels.

In fact many of the places where white girls could work in China were well known – from the Hotel Asia and the Kazbek in Canton, the Mascot Hotel in Chefoo (which also had a branch in Dairen), the Café Mukden and the China Eastern Railway Hotel in Mukden, to the Hotel Moderne in Harbin. Girls came and went between these establishments and those outside China, across the Far East. Demand was always high, the madams and pimps were always busy and they did well out of the trade.

But by the late 1930s things were changing for Brana and Rosie, and not just because of the advance of the Japanese across the whole of the Far East, from Manchuria to Malaya. It seemed the trouble that had caused Michael Consiglio and Madam Leschinsky to flee the Badlands was worse than Brana had been led to believe. It just wouldn't go away. The police were sniffing around; gossip abounded, courtesy of a worthless old man who'd come down from Newchwang and spread the story about Rosie's dead girl and her money all over town. And then there was that interfering White Russian Dolbetchef, who wouldn't stop talking about the scandal. Dolbetchef was a fool, taking Japanese money and telling everyone that one day he'd lead the White Russians back to Russia and restore the Tsar. Too many people poking their nose in, none of it good for business.

By the end of the decade, Brana's was reportedly one of the last brothels left in the Badlands. It was officially off limits to Western soldiers, by order of their legations, but since it had White Russian girls there were Japanese soldiers queuing up for the privilege. Brana and Rosie just had to pay off the Kempeitai, or military police, make sure the Russian pimps like Saxsen supplied enough girls, then sit back and count their money. War or no war, there were always men who wanted a brothel – it was the way of the world. Brana and Rosie didn't invent the business, they just went to work regardless of who ran Peking, regardless of who showed up at the door on Chuanpan Hutong.

What became of Brana and Rosie eventually remains a mystery. As always, rumours swirled: the pair had fled back to Tientsin, or had disappeared into the backstreets of Shanghai's Frenchtown, or posed as refugees and got themselves visas out, winding up – depending on the rumour – in San Francisco, Melbourne, Sao Paulo, someplace else. Perhaps the pestilential International Refugee

Camp at Tubabao in the Philippines, which in 1949 housed five thousand White Russian refugees from China, before they could be farmed out to America, Australia, Canada or South America.

One thing seems more certain – that Brana and Rosie did not go back to Bessarabia, where they'd started out as exploited girls around the turn of the century. And wherever it was they ended up, it seems they did not advertise their pasts.

Hong Kong's Lyndhurst Terrace

WHISKER'S GIRL HOUSE.

No. 1. Ki Siang Lane. Wei Hai Wei.
with.
Peiping Nice Girl
Chefoo Nice Girl
Tientsin Nice Girl
Shanghai Nice Girl
Hong Kong Nice Girl
Price Moderate & Situated in
A Sanitary Place:

號一里祥吉

Whisker's catered for all tastes

The Russian Pimp
Saxsen the Kot

axsen was a man without one single redeeming feature. He was the Badlands' number one *kot* – a Russian pimp, just about the lowest of the low. Pimps are a special kind of criminal. It's rarely a path taken out of desperation, and it doesn't require any great courage. Pimps are born, not made – a man's either a pimp or he's not, he's either able or not to live on the earnings of women forced to have sex with men not of their choosing. Should a woman dislike the client her pimp has found, well, too bad, she had to do it. Should she fall too ill to work, well, that was too bad also. A few slaps, punches and kicks would reinforce her position soon enough, and if that failed the pimp could always ensure she slept on the street.

Saxsen the *kot's* means of ensuring his girls went to work and didn't try to leave him was the needle and the pill. Nobody liked him – not the girls, not the madams, nor the clients, who he also scared. His dope dealer put up with him because he bought so much, on-selling to his girls and clients. When a girl hit rock bottom, there was Saxsen waiting to help her, with a broken-toothed smile, a client and drugs.

Who was he? Nobody knew for sure. Nobody ever even recorded his first name, if indeed they ever knew it – Saxsen wasn't a man with a lot of friends. He was probably a Volga German, a Russian with an ancient Germanic ancestry. He probably came from the city of Saratov. People said he'd got into some trouble with the police back there, pimping probably. Whatever his background, Saxsen was despised.

Saxsen quickly joined the army to get out of town, since *kots* didn't get treated too well in Russian jails. He seems to have been a veteran of the First World War, where he was conscripted into the Tsarist army. Rumour had it he deserted, fleeing Russia and the front to head eastwards to China. By the time he reached the Badlands he'd sunk low, and was said to have a long criminal record in both Russia and China. But maybe he just talked up his reputation in order to seem tough and keep the predators at bay, the sharks who might want his girls and his customers.

When Brana Shazker and Rosie Gerbert set up on Chuanpan Hutong they needed a protector. They found Saxsen waiting to help them. The women knew what Saxsen was but they had need of his services – freelancing wasn't an option in the Badlands. At least he wasn't a ponce; he didn't feign love for the girls whose earnings he lived off. In the hierarchy of the Badlands a *kot* was higher than a ponce, if not much else. With Saxsen it was business, pure and simple – he brought the girls customers, protected them, and sold dope to them and anyone else.

Saxsen liked his girls to be on the needle. It kept them loyal and allowed them to service a dozen or more clients a night, outdoors or indoors, since they didn't feel the cold or the pain and they'd do anything to get the next hit. Inevitably he was a user himself, and was thin and straggly, with bad nerves and nails that were bitten to the quick. His teeth were rotten from smoking filthy *papirosy* – thin, hand-rolled cigarettes made with cheap tobacco – his breath stank, his clothes were threadbare, he hardly ever ate.

But Saxsen was well connected and well positioned. He had rooms at number 29 Chuanpan Hutong, right next to Brana's brothel, so he knew all the girls and could easily deal heroin and pills along the strip, in and out of the bars and cabarets, delivering straight to any flophouse or rented room in the Badlands. When his girls needed a place to crash they stayed with him. He did most of his business out of the all-night Fu Sheng Restaurant across the road, and bought dope exclusively from the American Joe Knauf. Knauf dealt out of a flophouse he controlled, but he never openly sold himself.

Saxsen was hardly ever seen in daylight – a *kot* never came out before nightfall. His world was the small area between his flop-house, the Fu Sheng, a few clubs along Chuanpan and Hougou hutongs, and Knauf's place on the eastern edge of the Badlands. Nobody could recall ever having seen him outside the Badlands, although he did send his girls to entertain at parties in the Legation Quarter, and sometimes Joe Knauf set him up with a sweet deal to supply girls for 'gentlemen's weekends'. These were held at a temple rented by associates of Knauf's in the Western Hills, and they paid well, covering a car out and back for the girls. Saxsen would have liked to deal the dope there too, but since the men were pals of Knauf's it was his territory. And you didn't cross Joe Knauf unless you wanted trouble.

Saxsen also sent his girls to stag nights for bachelors from the Legation Quarter who came slumming it in the Badlands, and to parties for groups of soldiers about to be rotated out of Peking. But business was down by late 1937, with foreigners leaving town or going broke. When the Japanese had occupied Peking in July of that year they'd accelerated their strategy of flooding the city with narcotics in order to weaken Chinese resistance. More dope than ever was shipped in for sale in the city, now without any controls, and once the market was saturated, prices tumbled and addicts became legion. The Japanese military sat back and watched their plan working. High-grade opium was brought in from Iran; heroin and morphine came by train from factories in Korea, via Japanese-occupied Manchuria.

Within six months of taking Peking, the Japanese military had a hundred authorised drug shops up and running, and three hundred opium dens 'licensed' to sell Iranian opium at a discount. Tokyo was effectively subsidising drug addiction in China. Prices had soared in early 1937, after the Peking police tried to crack down and began arresting addicts and dealers and closing dens, and then they plummeted a year later as the market was flooded. Come late 1938, narcotics were so cheap and plentiful and addicts so common that pawnshops across Peking were encouraging their customers to take drugs rather than money for their goods; the proprietors rented syringes on the spot.

By 1939, after two years of occupation, Saxsen was almost destitute. He had nothing left to support himself with besides a little dealing to the dwindling number of foreigners left around the Badlands, and still the price kept falling. Even Joe Knauf had to buy his dope from the Japanese now, since alternative suppliers were not allowed – another reason for the price collapse. And Saxsen had only two girls left working for him on the streets, and they both had serious drug and alcohol habits, making them more and more erratic.

With the exception of the Japanese, times were tough for everyone in the Badlands. Look closely at the hustlers, the dope dealers, the porno card salesmen and the *kots* and you'd see suits shiny with wear and thinning at the elbows, their collars greasy, their cuffs frayed. The rake-thin dopers had an anaemic yellow tinge to their skin; the girls and the older whores had dry scaly skin under their cheap, plastered-on makeup. The smoke-and-mirrors trick that was the Badlands by night – when aging women and unhealthy girls were lit by low-watt fish-skin lamps or by candles, with shadows to hide the worst defects – vanished in the bright glare of daylight. The Badlands and its denizens were coming apart at the seams.

And so Saxsen did what he'd done before whenever things got tough – in Saratov, at the front – he packed a bag and left, skipping on his rent in Chuanpan Hutong. His table at the Fu Sheng sat empty, his two remaining girls were left to fend for themselves. Where he went and what became of him is not known. Perhaps, like so many Badlands refugees, he made it to Shanghai but found the war, chaos and poverty overwhelming and decided to end it all, slashing his wrists in a Frenchtown boarding house or overdosing in a shack-cum-brothel in the Hongkew Trenches.

Perhaps his weakened body limped on, into an insane asylum that catered for dope addicts, or a charitable sanatorium for indigent whites. Or maybe, at the end of the war, a United Nations camp, as one of the many thousands of undocumented displaced persons in China, the detritus of war's aftermath. Or perhaps he got himself a new identity, a new passport, a new life. Perhaps . . . But it's just speculation. The truth is he too vanished. Saxsen was swallowed up by history, becoming another unwanted relic of a sordid past that had no place in postwar China.

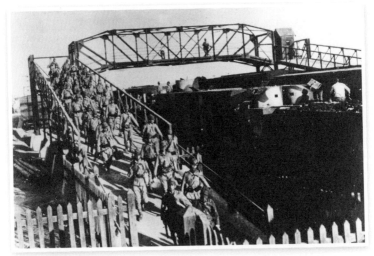

Japanese troops arriving in Peking, August 1937

Occupying troops patrolling Peking's streets

The Girls
Marie and Peggy

Some girls turn to prostitution because they're destitute, some because it beats spending fourteen hours a day on your feet in a factory or a department store and getting varicose veins, and some, like Brana and Rosie, because they're tricked into it. One day a man they think loves them puts a knife to their throat and tells them to service his friends and give him the money.

And then there are girls like Marie, who was taken to a Badlands brothel by her father, introduced to a man with rotten teeth and foul breath, and told to let him and the others do what they wanted. At not quite thirteen years of age, Marie was left there. Her father, in return, was given a cut of her earnings.

As a young girl Marie hadn't known much beyond a filthy back room in a Japanese-owned boarding house in a notorious slum known as Yang-I Hutong, in Peking's Eastern City. She shared a toilet with fifteen other penniless White Russian families and subsisted on dry bread and tea, along with several hundred of Peking's most desperate stateless White Russians.

Her mother had died, or run away, before she could remember.

Her father was a drunk, and a nasty one at that, addicted to cheap vodka. As soon as Marie hit puberty she was sold to the man with the bad teeth and worse breath, and pretty quickly she worked out what she was, what she'd become.

Most of the women in the brothel were older than Marie and not kind. They, like plenty of older prostitutes elsewhere, resented the younger girls because they reminded them of their age, reminded them they would soon be finished in the trade. They knew that their customers would see the young girls and want them; that those girls would get the work, the money, the little treats that occasionally came a working girl's way. And because the younger ones earnt more, they were treated better than the older women, by the madams and the pimps and the brothel staff, from the muscle on the door to the Chinese skivvy that took the pisspots away. Youth and freshness were currency in a prostitute's world, age and time the enemy. The older women hated Marie.

So she made friends with another new girl, Peggy, only a couple of years older than herself and also a White Russian. Peggy had grown up in the city of Harbin, in Manchuria, which had the largest White Russian community outside Shanghai, and she was from a solid family. They were down on their luck after having to leave Russia, but they still had a house, a fire in the grate, and food. With her two younger sisters, Peggy sat at a table for dinner every night. Her father worked as a clerk in a Russian business that traded along the border with Mongolia and Russia. The family went to church in the onion-domed Saint Sophia Cathedral, and Peggy attended bible classes under the stern gaze of Father Shelaeff. In winter she ice-skated on the Sunggari River with her Russian classmates.

Peggy liked school, she liked learning and reading and studying, and when she was fifteen she discovered she also liked boys. Harbin had a lot of Russian boys with blue eyes and fair skin, who played sports and boxed and skated, and had bright wide smiles and rows of white teeth.

There was one boy in particular. Peggy knew he wasn't suitable; she knew that his family was considered to be trouble – a family from the city of Khabarovsk, all of whose sons were under the sway of their criminal father. They were never mentioned in polite Russian houses in Harbin, but they were gossiped about in the bars. It was Peggy's misfortune to fall in love with this boy, who then introduced her to a man who forced himself upon her while her boyfriend watched and laughed. Afterwards, the man paid her boyfriend and spat on Peggy.

Shamed and unable to return home, she was handed over by her boyfriend, for a fee, to a Russian female pimp, a *bandersha*, who recruited girls for White Russian brothels across China. Peggy was subsequently sold to Madam Leschinsky's brothel on Chuanpan Hutong. She was no longer a respectable schoolgirl from Harbin who went to Father Shelaeff's Sunday school, she was a trafficked girl who made her money on her back.

There was a time, before 1937, while they were still young, when Marie and Peggy were the twin beauties of the Badlands. Rich Westerners who came slumming it from the Legation Quarter would pay for both of them simultaneously. The pair had known each other so long – protecting each other from the spiteful older women, who loved to find an excuse to rake their fingernails down the girls' cheeks and ruin their looks, to claw their chests so that no man would dream of their bosoms – that they were quite comfortable touching each other. There was nothing in it, just work, and big tips behind Madam Leschinsky's back. Marie and Peggy were best friends; they looked out for each other.

They didn't look like twins, though. Marie, a Siberian, was fair-skinned and freckled, a quick learner. Peggy was darker, almost Latin; the punters thought she was Italian, and some of them thought she had a screw loose. She had a dreadful temper, in fact, and would periodically lose it, with clients, with Leschinsky and Consiglio, with the older women in the brothel. She'd once smashed up the Oparinas' dive bar next door, when their dirty-minded son Yashka tried it on. She invariably got slapped by Consiglio for her fits. Only Marie could calm her down. Peggy was a good earner, so the house tolerated her – to a point.

But during those good times, Marie and Peggy rarely rose much before two in the afternoon, after which they went out walking and window-shopping, snacking and gossiping – two working girls who liked to practise their English because they thought it might come in useful. Marie reputedly became almost fluent. They'd wander up to Morrison Street, just this side of the Legation Quarter, to the expensive department stores and hotels. They liked to dawdle outside the Grand Hôtel de Pékin and watch the tourists passing through, and see the smart American and European ladies of the Quarter arriving for tiffin. They loved to see the latest fashions from London or Paris, the furs from Siberia, and would gaze in the window of The Camel Bell next door, the most fashionable shop in all Peking. Run by an American woman, it specialised in furs, *Chinois*-style dresses and curios.

They could only look, though; they knew two Russian working girls wouldn't be welcome for tiffin in the hotel, or be allowed to try on the beautiful dresses and furs, or admire the knick-knacks for sale. So they would hurry back to Hatamen Street, to where a Jewish-Russian tailor from Odessa had his shop, and describe to him what they had just seen on the Legation Quarter women. The tailor would then run them up cheap imitations, making Marie and Peggy the most fashionable girls working the Badlands.

Further up on Hatamen Street they bought the tools of their trade – condoms, in boxes of a gross, from a small shop run by a Jewish refugee from Europe who also specialised in perfumes, lilac water, peroxide dyes, and the newfangled permanent-wave kits. Under the counter he sold Blue Unction, a grease that could burn your skin if you used too much, but which killed the crabs and lice the girls got repeatedly from the dirty sheets and the customers.

There were some White Russian Girls working in the Legation Quarter, doing permanents and manicures in Violeta's Beauty Parlour. But the owner, a Moscow woman who liked to pass herself off as French, would spot Peggy and Marie as the wrong sort of working girl and either ignore them or throw them out. So instead they went to a beauty parlour on Yang-I Hutong, which was really a converted living room. They could never afford Sennet Frerés, the Legation Quarter jewellers, and their lack of money also meant they never had their photo taken together at the Hartung Studio, as they longed to.

Sometimes, on these afternoon excursions, Marie would see her father. But they didn't talk; he didn't even recognise her, though her body still paid for his drink. The man was a wreck by now, incontinent, reduced to drinking the *samogon* brewed by an old man from Kazan in a Yang-I Hutong yard, and reputed to have sent half a dozen men blind.

The other thing that drew Peggy and Marie outdoors was food. They loved the teeming Dong'an Market, which spilled along the ancient hutongs to the east of Morrison Street. And on early spring or summer evenings they could be seen walking arm in arm along Chuanpan and Hougou hutongs up to Soochow Hutong, for sweet candied hawthorns on sticks from the Chinese vendors, or tasty *yangrou chuan* – mutton on sticks. If they'd come into a decent tip from a customer, they might walk on to the French patisserie on Hatamen Street for cream cakes, or to Shikin's Russian Bakery for hot *pirozhki*, buns glazed with egg and filled with cabbage. Once in a while they'd go to the Tung Tan Restaurant, down near the junction of Hatamen Street and Chang'an Avenue, which did a roaring trade serving Chinese food to a largely Western crowd. Peggy and Marie would ignore the stares and giggles of the young men from the more respectable side of foreign Peking, who would point out the Badlands girls but didn't have the nerve to talk to them.

The nights could be hard. The customers were sometimes violent, often drunk and dirty, and there might be six, seven, eight of them a night – double that on weekends and holidays. Men didn't linger at Madam Leschinsky's; it wasn't a bordello, there were no refinements. The rooms stunk, and were typically bare but for an iron bedstead with an old mattress, a small table and chair for the man to hang his clothes over, a jug of water and a bowl, an ashtray, a single light bulb with no shade. The windows were never opened, the sheets rarely changed. Marie and Peggy had to keep their meagre belongings in old suitcases slipped under the beds along with the reeking chamber pots, which were emptied only at the end of the night. The jerry-built brothels of the Badlands were completely infested: stink bugs dropped from the ceilings onto the beds, centipedes and scorpions lurked, infuriating 'feather bugs' could be heard scratching behind the tattered wallpaper all night.

Soldiers were regulars at the brothel – US Marines, the Queen's Royal West Surreys, Italian Marine Guards. The place was technically off limits to them but they came anyway. They didn't care about the lack of decoration or the infestations. It was only a short walk from the US Marine barracks at the American Legation, down the Chienmen end of the Quarter, to the Badlands. The European barracks were even closer. Most of the men went first to the Oparinas' dive next door, to get up their Dutch courage or to buy cheap sets of porno cards from the salesmen who prowled the bar.

Other customers were pulled in off the street by Saxsen, who was always out looking for work for his girls. If the men came via the Oparinas, then the money was handled by Leschinsky or Consiglio, and later, Rosie Gerbert, with Saxsen getting a cut. If Saxsen brought in the business direct, then he saw Consiglio right. At the end of a long night Marie and Peggy would get their portion in the Fu Sheng opposite.

They rarely saw the customers' faces. They'd see a shape, a form, the clothes, which were often a uniform, but they didn't look at the faces. The men never knocked before entering the room, not seeing any need to respect a girl like Peggy or Marie. They would undress themselves, although Marie would help unbutton their trousers so she could surreptitiously look for the telltale sores that said a man was syphilitic.

She'd put a condom on them; while some men would refuse to wear one, the soldiers mostly didn't object. Marie wasn't their first prostitute and they had wives or sweethearts at home they wanted to go back to clean. There was no standing on ceremony – this was a place to come for sex and then leave. For that reason it was rarely a long process, although occasionally the drink meant they needed a little coaxing. Some clients were easily pleased with simple things, some wanted stranger stuff.

Their business done, they wiped themselves off, pissed in her chamber pot, dressed and went out. The encounter was mostly silent, the men saying nothing; Marie usually didn't know their language anyway. They paid downstairs, Leschinsky in the old days, or Rosie. Some might toss a coin or two her way by means of a tip.

When they'd gone, Marie would have a few precious moments before the next client. She sat listening to the faint music from the Oparinas' gramophone next door, the sounds from downstairs and from the other upstairs bedrooms, and the all-night clamour of the hutong outside – rickshaws, cars, crowds of soldiers shouting, the clanging pots of the snack sellers passing by. She'd daydream momentarily of those lovely dresses in The Camel Bell, the white linen tablecloths of the Grand Hôtel de Pékin's tiffin, and of other lives she might one day live. Maybe she'd move to Shanghai or Tientsin, to a better house, a kinder madam. She'd think about what she and Peggy might do tomorrow, where they might go. Then another man would walk in and it all began again.

Then one night, when the brothel was packed with Italian Marines out on leave, drunk and stinking of boozy sweat but fast in bed, Marie, Peggy and the other girls heard terrible screams. After that they were confined to their rooms with the doors locked. They could hear comings and goings all night, Leschinsky and Consiglio arguing, shouting and screaming. Then the girls were all let go, pushed out onto the street, just like that. The Shantung strong-arm guys barred the doors after them. Madam Leschinsky and Michael Consiglio had already gone, the girls were told. The rumour was they'd skipped town, disappeared to Tientsin, or maybe Shanghai's Frenchtown.

Over the road at the Fu Sheng, Marie and Peggy tried to think what to do next. Then Saxsen came in and found them and they became his girls, moving into his rooms next door to their old place of work.

But now they had to work the street, taking customers to rooms in the flophouses on Hougou Hutong, which were even worse than Madam Leschinsky's. The fleas and bugs were more prevalent, and the customers seemed worse here too. There was trouble from the ones who didn't want to pay, and the 'kinks' – men who wanted weird stuff – were more regular now.

After they'd done their job they had to leave the room quickly. It was hard to clean yourself in those flophouses; there was only cold water to douche with and often it was dirty, so they got infections from that too. Pretty soon Peggy and Marie started to look scruffy, and there was no longer time for the beautician or the dressmaker. Saxsen was taking more and more of their money, his cut growing as their desperation increased. Marie and Peggy were in no position to argue. Being out on the streets, they couldn't charge as much as they had before, and their chance at a secure life and a regular place to stay was slipping away. They didn't go up to Hatamen Street now, to the patisserie or for *pirozhki*. Mostly they just ate cheap greasy noodles in the Fu Sheng, along with the dealers, the dopers, and the other working girls, who were constantly harassed by their pimps trying to get them back on the street.

The awning outside the Fu Sheng saw huddles of more hustlers, Chinese mostly – rickshaw men, fences looking to buy stolen goods, moneylenders recognising the desperation of the foreigners with addictions and others who'd reached the end of their rope. Local kids would stand watch over the few cars that came into the Badlands, and scramble madly for coins from the odd swell slumming it on Chuanpan Hutong, who'd occasionally hurl pennies over their shoulder.

That winter of 1937 was long and cold, seemingly without end. Business was down; people said war was coming, the Japs were coming. And Saxsen expected Peggy and Marie to service more customers than ever. As things got tougher, Marie would often be out of it; she'd go for an early evening's drinking in the Oparinas' bar, or take Saxsen's heroin pills. One night she was so cold that she let Saxsen inject her – immediate oblivion and warmth.

After that she could spend a night in the flophouse and never notice the cold, or feel the fleas bite. She didn't look in a mirror and see how dry her skin was, how her scalp was flaking and her hair a mess. She took heroin again and again; it dulled the pain of the work, the stink of the customers. Saxsen brought soldiers to the rooms, three, four, five at a time, but Marie was numb to it all.

Peggy, too, was led by the harshness of life in the flophouses to Saxsen's heroin, his injections and his pills. Her mind started to go, and she drank to stop the devils in her head, but that just made them worse. Whereas at Madam Leschinsky's she'd spend all her spare time with Marie, now she was mostly alone, since they worked out of different flophouses. She needed more and more alcohol but had less money, so she started drinking the *samogon* from the illegal stills of Yang-I Hutong.

Her fits got worse, her temper shredded and she'd turn manic, fighting customers, flophouse landlords, the Japanese soldiers who'd started venturing into the Badlands, anyone in her path when she was seeing red. Eventually customers began to avoid her foulmouthed rants and she sank ever further.

When Peking was finally occupied Marie and Peggy, in their stupors, hardly noticed. Saxsen upped sticks and disappeared, leaving Marie, by now an addict, without a regular source of heroin or permanent lodgings. She moved from flophouse to flophouse, paying day by day. If she turned enough tricks she'd get a room for the night, and maybe some pills to help her sleep. If not then she had to bunk somewhere or sleep on the street, and go without her fix. Marie now had access to only the most adulterated heroin, cut with strychnine and flour. She shared and reused rented needles until they were blunt and left puncture wounds and bruises on her arms, on the backs of her legs, the insides of her thighs. She lost touch with Peggy, who was fighting her own dope and drink demons in other flophouses.

It was not a long-term proposition. In the summer of 1939, Shura Giraldi, the mysterious *éminence grise* of the Peking Badlands who'd known Marie since her arrival there, commented, 'She just rolls her eyes and opens and shuts her mouth as she wags her head from side to side; she is finished; can hardly live a fortnight longer.'

And she didn't. Before summer was over Marie took an overdose of heroin and died. Whether intentionally or not is unknown. She was not yet thirty.

With Saxsen gone and Marie lost to her, Peggy had sunk into her own pit of heroin and cheap rotgut. Her mood swings and mental state became worse as she continued to self-medicate, but around the time Marie overdosed, Peggy managed somehow to get herself back to Harbin – the rumour mill said Shura paid the train fare. There, estranged from her family, who no longer wanted to know her, she was reduced to living in the notorious Hotel Moderne, and then day-rate flophouses catering to poor transients.

In that freezing northern city she continued selling her body, for pennies and vodka. Though the details are now lost, it seems that eventually, during a violent drunken rage in a hotel room, Peggy was taken by the authorities and committed to an insane asylum, where she died some months later. Like Marie, she was at most thirty years old.

Grand Hôtel de Pékin - the best tiffin in Peking

Hatamen Street - the border between the Badlands and the Legation Quarter

Advertising hoardings close to the Badlands, 1930s

The Dealer
Bad Joe Knauf's Business and Blades

merican-born Joe Knauf was short and squat and hairy, with a pronounced Roman nose that everyone commented on behind his back. He lived in a dump of a lodging house on the eastern edge of the Badlands, from where he traded in dope and women, and he was universally disliked.

The lodging house was a shithole. Ripped paper in the window frames let in chilling breezes in winter, and it was stiflingly airless in the humid summer months, but it didn't seem to bother him. Visitors would often find him dressed in nothing but a silk kimono, and at other times he'd stand naked and high as a kite in the building's courtyard, not a stitch on and waving a big Bowie fighting knife around. He had been arrested for this behaviour several times.

The internal courtyard, onto which the back rooms of the building faced, was permanently plunged into dank shadow. From it emanated the stink of rotting vegetables and human waste, rising up from the collective midden. In the summer it was overpowering. Who knew when or how it ever got cleared.

Despite its rundown state, the building was perfectly located for

Knauf's business – close to Chuanpan Hutong and within minutes of every major venue in the Badlands. Inside, it was a rabbit warren of more long shadows and dark corridors, where the doors were locked and unlocked constantly, where people were always coming and going. Whispers, mutterings, deals done, packages delivered, parcels removed, occasionally a shouted argument, the constant banging of doors. The sound of Chinese, English, Korean and Japanese being spoken, all mixed up. In the rooms, curtains were permanently drawn to block out the street outside; dust mites were visible in the occasional shafts of light.

Dirty bare floorboards, peeling paint, long-dead light bulbs – the place was in such a severe state of disrepair that some people dreaded going in there. Nobody knew who actually owned it, but it was said the Chinese landlords had let Knauf take control of the whole building, so scared were they of his violent outbursts and his connections with the Japanese. His little Korean girl – his 'slave', as he liked to call her – doubled as the building's skivvy, emptying the chamber pots onto the midden, carrying water, and bringing food from the nearby Fu Sheng Restaurant.

Joe Knauf was a dedicated knife man and he liked to display his blade. He would remove it from the scabbard on his belt, wipe it on his sleeve, on his thigh, then hold it up to his face and twirl it, letting everyone know what he was carrying. People rightly feared Knauf and his knife. The man was a former US Marine, sticky and solid. He might have been short but that gave him a low centre of gravity, and he had reach, with arms like a monkey's. He was ideally built to be a knife fighter, with plenty of muscle on his arms, chest and neck – to his opponents it appeared as though any blade of theirs would break off on him.

Moreover he had a dangerous glint in his eye, a look that told people to back off, to keep away. He was unpredictable and volatile, likely to explode into violence at any moment. Joe Knauf, it was said, liked to see death close up. He was known to go regularly to the Tien Chiao public execution grounds, along with some of his Badlands cronies, to watch the death sentences being carried out. Nowadays these were done by bullet rather than the more elaborate stranglings of earlier times. This was enough to send a chill down many people's spines – the horrific and ghoulish Tien Chiao was not somewhere many foreigners ever ventured.

Women instinctively hated him on sight, men were wary of him. Even Saxsen the pimp kept out of his way except when buying dope from him. Rickshaw pullers put their heads down and ignored him; they knew he would dicker them on the fare and he never tipped. If they complained he was likely to pull his knife. The girls of the Badlands avoided him too, as far as possible. Marie and Peggy dreaded him coming into Madam Leschinsky's with his creepy pals, waving his knife in their faces like he owned the place. Joe Knauf was quite simply bad news all over the Badlands, but he had a coterie based on his dope. The poor Korean girl lived in terror of him, but stayed because she was an addict.

Within the Badlands there were circles within circles. While most of the joints were run by White Russians, the actual premises were usually owned by wealthy Chinese who had nothing to do with what went on day to day in the venues. They just collected the rent and looked the other way. Licences were a different matter; these were owned by a mix of rich Chinese – often overseas Chinese, with money and businesses in London, California or Paris – and a few foreigners.

Networks were formed, associations made, and not always the most obvious ones. It wasn't uncommon to find that respectable, professional foreigners – long-term residents of the city, members in good standing at the Legation Quarter's most exclusive clubs, who with their wives were given the best tables in the swankiest hotels – were also silent partners in Badlands nightclubs and bars. These men knew the likes of Joe Knauf and Saxsen, who weren't members in good standing of anything, and who wouldn't be shown to the best tables anywhere outside a cheap Badlands joint. The Italian doctor Ugo Capuzzo, who owned the Roma Nightclub and cinema on the North Settlement Area's Chang'an Avenue, was known as a man who liked to frequent the Badlands when not treating his upscale patients in the Legation Quarter. The seemingly above board mixed with the decidedly low life right there on Chuanpan and Hougou hutongs, in the nightclubs and the seedy flophouse bedrooms that girls like Marie and Peggy were reduced to working in.

Circles within circles, ever downwards, like Dante's inferno, until they touched the bottom of pure wickedness and evil. Knauf liked to mix with like-minded Americans and with Europeans from both the Badlands and the Legation Quarter, but he didn't have much time for the Russians, who he treated as second-class citizens. He kept in tight with the Japanese and the Koreans, since they supplied his dope and now also ran Peking, and he spoke a smattering of both languages. After July 1937 the American Legation opened a file on him as a possible collaborator.

Since walking away from the Marines, Knauf had barely left the Badlands, except on hunting trips to the Western Hills. In the mid-1930s the American Legation noted that he was running a brothel with Madam Oparina, of Chuanpan Hutong dive-bar fame, until they fell out. Knauf managed the Olympic Theatre for a while, but that ended when he got rough with one too many customers – that sort of behaviour was bad for business, and Chang'an Avenue wasn't quite the rough-and-tumble of the Badlands proper.

Knauf had also pimped girls out around the Badlands, and for a while, in the wilder days of the local warlords around Peking, he'd dealt in arms and ammunition too, activities that had first brought him to the attention of the American Legation. He was a heavy drinker and a drug taker and was generally unwilling to reason with anyone. His immediate circle was a bunch of ex-US Marines who'd quit the army, or in a few cases been kicked out.

The group included Michael Consiglio, Madam Leschinsky's brothel partner, who was not afraid of a brawl himself. Half Italian, half Filipino, he had been thrown out of the Marines for disorderly conduct. Arthur Ringwalt, an American diplomat in Peking at the time, described Consiglio as 'ferocious and cruel'. There was also Thomas Jack, an Italian-born naturalised American who had taken a most un-Italian name. Like Consiglio he'd been hired into the Marines in China, rather than sent out from the States, and these 'local hires' were always seen as the dregs.

Jack had quit the Marines and bummed around the Badlands, working as a mechanic officially, but unofficially involved in the nightclub business and running dope for Knauf. Knauf, Consiglio and Jack liked to drink together with the other ex-Marines who hung around the area. They helped each other out, using their position and contacts to sell dope to current Marines at the American Legation, and after Knauf was sacked from the Olympic Theatre he still managed to get Jack a position there.

Knauf always conducted his dope dealing from the rooms at his flophouse, which had only one phone line with one telephone, which only Knauf ever answered. Customers would come to the front gate, which was solid iron and four metres high, with a small, head-height gap through which to see who was outside. If Knauf's boy knew them he'd let them in. If he didn't know them he waited for Knauf to look out the upstairs window and nod them in.

The dope was kept stacked, weighed and ready to go in various rooms, the doors of which were always locked. They were then unlocked, opened, the dope handed over and the cash received, before the doors were closed and locked again. Knauf kept girls, a mix of Korean, Russian and Chinese, in most of the rooms to watch over the drugs and the money – it seems he trusted them not to steal the latter or use the former.

The Korean gangsters who collaborated with the Japanese and brought heroin into China were rewarded with permission to deal it. They kept the stuff pretty pure at first; the Japanese wanted it that way so as to get people hooked, sap their will to resist. Opium, which had been traded in China for a century and a half, was still being brought in, but the rituals around it, the pipes, the recliners and dens, all took time. The Japanese wanted drugs that were quick and easy to manufacture, distribute and consume, so through the 1930s heroin was dealt too, along with needles – the 'works' – to inject it. The more dope could be moved across the entire country, creating masses of addicts, the more quickly the Japanese military high command felt it could conquer the whole of China.

The dopers wanted quick hits too, and cheaply – dope prices might be down but so were earnings. Times were tight. After the Japanese took Peking they didn't bother bringing in pure dope any more, they brought 'red pills' instead, courtesy of Japanese-run factories in Korea and Manchuria.

These heroin pills, which were cut with caffeine, quinine, sugar and strychnine, and even brick dust, had first appeared in the 1920s in Shanghai. Taken orally, they were an easy fix, and compared to smoking opium they were stronger, more addictive and, for Knauf, easier to store and to shift on the streets. The profit margin was greater than for straight-up opium too, and there wasn't the clumsy business of needles or pipes, although the pills could still be smoked if desired, using a less elaborate form of a hookah consisting of a kind of vase with a bamboo straw inserted through a small hole in the side. The Japanese supplied the pills, the Japanese policed the streets of Peking now – it was an open business, Knauf effectively had a free hand and a licence to deal.

Addicts got through these new pills rapidly. They died in large numbers as they overdosed, wasted away, got poisoned, or contracted gangrene in open sores, all caused by badly cut pills. Throughout the Badlands in 1939 and 1940, the smell of opium gave way to the telltale smell of the red pills – burnt sugar. Opium went mostly to the dens, where pipes were still prepared for the more discerning smokers. Knauf's dealers, men like Saxsen, fanned out across the Badlands selling red pills an ounce at a time. A pill was known by its American slang name – a 'Cadillac'.

In 1941, when dopers were rounded up along with other foreigners, they were suddenly living alongside more respectable families. According to Langdon Gilkey, whose Weihsien memoir *Shantung Compound* has remained the most vivid and detailed portrait of life in the camp, there were 'two jazz musicians (a Polynesian and a negro) housed with a Belgian dope addict; and beyond them were a British banker, an engineer, and the China head of the Asiatic Petroleum Company'. In internment the Legation Quarter and the Badlands finally came side by side in the daylight.

But there were also plenty of Badlands residents who didn't get sent to camps, because they'd become traitors to their countries – of either birth or adoption. They took the Japanese side and remained free, turning the Badlands into a multinational den of collaborators. Joe Knauf's name doesn't show up on any records of those arrested and detained after Pearl Harbor. It seems he remained in the Badlands, at liberty to sell his opium and heroin and pills to anyone, Chinese or foreign, left to buy.

Rumour had it he died sometime around late 1944 or early 1945, of complications arising from sampling too much of his own product, or perhaps from alcoholism, food shortages, the cold weather, a fatal dose of pneumonia . . . Nothing was recorded of his fate at the American Legation, because that had been shut and locked up. Nothing was recorded anywhere; nobody, it seems, mourned his passing. Joe Knauf, the nasty knife man of the Badlands, disappeared like a puff of his own opium smoke. There one minute, gone the next, and missed by absolutely no one.

The King of the Badlands
The Enigma that was
Shura Giraldi

hatever anyone declared categorically about Shura Giraldi, someone else insisted on the exact opposite. Shura was a man, Shura was a woman.
Shura was handsome and beautiful, Shura was a
freak of nature and a pervert. Shura was kind and good, Shura was
exploitative and evil. Shura was just another struggling White Russian refugee trying to get by, of no real consequence save as a gossip
and a sexual curiosity; Shura was the heart and brains of a gang that
ran clubs, whores, illicit booze and drugs, when not robbing banks
and stealing gems to fence in Shanghai.

Shura moved Zelig-like across the seedy landscape of interwar
Peking, all things to all men – and women – sometimes an anony-
mous man in a suit lost in a crowd, sometimes an eye-catching,
head-turning femme fatale in a tailored dress with ruby-red nails,
jet-black hair, and a smile that could melt a man's heart at forty
paces. Shura was nothing if not an enigma.

In his memoirs of 1930s Peking, Englishman John Blofeld remembers Shura as a slightly down-at-heel Badlands bar habitué in
a dive called the Kavkaz, trading chit-chat among a smattering of

washed-up Russian whores who were speaking bad French in order to sound classy and drinking cheap Georgian brandy to obliterate their depression at having precious few customers. Others recall the Kavkaz as Shura's joint, the base of his multifarious lucrative activities in China, criminal and semi-criminal.

In the archives of the Shanghai Municipal Police, and in popular White Russian legend across China, Shura was the mastermind of the largest ever bank heist in Chinese history, the raid on the Bank of Peking in the spring of 1937, from which not a single cent, penny, dollar or yuan of any denomination was ever recovered. The robbers got clean away, and if Shura *was* the mastermind, then there's no one left alive now to tell the truth of that raid or where the money went.

The police also thought he was probably a cunning jewel thief, using as mules gullible foreign women who fell for his charms. The women transported stolen gems to White Russian fences in the backstreets of Shanghai's Frenchtown, forging a connection between the badlands of Peking and Shanghai.

Even today, three-quarters of a century or more later, the remnants of Peking's old White Russian community that still survive across the globe – in San Francisco, Toronto, Melbourne, Rio de Janeiro and Hong Kong – disagree fervidly about who the real Shura was. One former Badlands habitué who contacted me after reading *Midnight in Peking,* an old man now living in Brazil who had been a stateless young White Russian in Peking in the 1930s, declared himself shocked that anyone should suggest the man he knew as 'Diadia Shura', or Uncle Shura, was a crook. He was nothing of the sort, according to the old man, just a slightly effeminate and somewhat shady teller of great anecdotes.

Another old White Russian woman, who fled with her family to Hong Kong in 1949 and still lives there, sent me a letter to say she was thrilled to hear the name Shura again in connection to the Bad-lands, the first time she had in more than sixty years. She told me she knew for sure that Shura had participated in every aspect of 1930s Peking – nightclubs, bars, brothels, burglaries, fencing stolen goods, drug dealing. This was 'common knowledge', she maintained.

And it was a White Russian family who'd been involved in the entertainment economy of the Badlands in various ways between the wars who described Shura to me, with great affection, as the 'King of the Badlands'. So where does the truth lie? Here's what we know, or think we know:

Shura Giraldi was a hermaphrodite, and used this quirk from a young age to switch from one sex to another as the mood or circum-stance took him. He was man or woman according to whichever best suited his purposes at any given moment. To avoid confusion, though, I'll refer to Shura as 'he'. His real name, his birth name, was prob-ably Alexander Mikhailovitch (aka Ivan, Vania, Vanushka) Sosnitsky. It seems he was born in the city of Tomsk, Siberia, to a father who was a middle-ranking Tsarist official, just before the turn of the last century. Tomsk had profited from the gold rush of 1830, but by the time Shura was born it had become a backwater. Bypassed by the Trans-Siberian Railway, which travelled through Novosibirsk instead, it was now a key centre of White resistance to Bolshevism. When Shura's father was murdered by the Bolsheviks, Shura joined a group of refugees fleeing eastwards.

He lived for a time in northern China, probably in the heavily Russified city of Harbin, or perhaps Mukden, before settling in Pe-king, where his rise to notoriety and legend status began. He took the name Shura early in life – Russian males named Alexander are often known as Sasha, females called Alexandra are often known as Shura. In the 1930s, when he met John Blofeld, a sensualist who had come to China to immerse himself in its ancient philosophies and religions, he declared to him: 'Me you will call Shura, as everyone does. Alexander Mikhailovitch? Who is he, no one know. Shura? All Peking know Shura.'

We know roughly what Shura looked like as a man in 1939, from an account of him given to the French Concession Police in Shanghai by E.T.C. Werner, who described him as 'between five-foot eight and five-foot ten in height, rather heavily built but not stout, with light-coloured hair but not blonde, and a pallid complexion. This person is probably in their forties, of Korean extraction but had rather indiscriminate racial features, and was said to be a hermaphrodite.' Earlier descriptions have him as slender, with dark or raven hair, of Siberian extraction with somewhat Asiatic eyes and cheekbones. And these descriptions are probably right too: Shura was a chameleon as well as an enigma.

Accounts of Shura as a woman describe a glamorous beauty in stunning dresses. The dancer Tatiana Korovina recalled him binding his breasts tightly in order to dress as a man, but when she saw him descend the stairs as a woman at his Paomachang house, he had 'pert breasts, almond eyes, perfectly formed and brilliantly white teeth'.

We know he lived at least some of the time in Yang-I Hutong, the overcrowded White Russian slum in the Chinese eastern portion of the Tartar City, and a far cry from his luxurious house in Paomachang. Yang-I Hutong seems to be where he came when he first arrived in Peking, penniless. Shura's social life, his business interests and his lovers were almost exclusively Russian, and so it's perhaps understandable that he would retain a place in this small ghetto of his countrymen.

When trouble loomed he would make the sign of the cross, in front of one of the Russian icons he always had on the walls of his bars, brothels and homes. He may not have been religious but he was, as criminals invariably are, superstitious. If the rumours of his unlawful life are true, then anonymity among the other stateless whites of Peking would have been useful. Shura didn't pop his head over the parapet – to the authorities he stayed largely under the radar.

And so the stories began. While some believed he was no more than the cashier at the Kavkaz, others, including John Blofeld, remember him as one of the largest wine dealers in Peking, and all out of the Kavkaz. And what other Badlands bar cashier had his own personal dance troupe? A troupe that performed not just across the Badlands, but in Shanghai and the Far East circuit. Surely no stateless Russian barman could possibly own a summerhouse overlooking the Paomachang Racecourse?

Any number of old White Russian China Hands remember Shura's Paomachang house, which was big enough for them to refer to it as a 'resort'. Many young men congregated there; Shura liked to have handsome boys around him. His boudoir was on the ground floor and was dominated by a huge bed supported by two carved black swans, with a backlit ceiling of painted silk to match his collection of tailored, figure-hugging silk cheongsams. It was a touch gaudy, but spectacular all the same. Here he would relax in black silk culottes in the humid summer, his petite feet shod in black cotton Chinese slippers of the type favoured by unskilled labourers and rickshaw pullers.

It was in this summer retreat, in the late 1920s, so rumour had it, that a Chinese warlord once begged Shura to marry him, and on discovering Shura's twin sex had fled into obscurity to avoid the shame and loss of face. It was widely believed that another of his lovers, in the 1930s, was a senior official in the Kuomintang administration in Peking – a man he affectionately called Zaichek, meaning 'little rabbit', or 'bunny'. It seems Zaichek made sure that Shura's investments in the Badlands were never looked at too closely, and that rumours of his involvement in bank heists and jewel robberies were never investigated with too much gusto. A very useful little rabbit indeed.

Shura had a piece of everything in the Badlands, so it was said. He had minor holdings, majority holdings; he bought and sold interests in Badlands joints all the time. Along with the rather dingy Russian-style Kavkaz and its traditional accordion music, best suited to maudlin émigrés who could never go home and who were looking to drown their sorrows, there was Marnac's French-style joint, decorated in the style of Toulouse-Lautrec, a *fin de siècle* can-can hall.

There was also the Olympic Theatre, which mimicked a sophisticated, white-walled Manhattan nightclub, and a brothel in a big building on the edge of the Badlands that was staffed exclusively with Korean girls. This building was owned by the Soviet Legation and rented by Shura and his lover at the time, a Russian jockey at Paomachang – not a deal a mere cashier in a bar could arrange. The brothel's customers were predominantly off-duty US Marines and Flying Tigers, as well as other soldiers on legation guard duty. It made a fortune.

Regardless of how he made his money, people mostly liked Shura Giraldi. Even the scholar-diplomat E.T.C. Werner surprisingly liked him, and he was hardly of that world. Shura knew everyone and everyone knew him in Peking's demi-monde – if the circles within circles of the Badlands had a central hub, it was Shura. He knew the fates of Leschinsky and Consiglio after they'd had to skip town, he knew the Oparinas, he knew the madams Brana Shazker and Rosie Gerbert, he knew the working girls Marie and Peggy. Tatiana Korovina danced in his troupe, Roy Tchoo managed the Olympic Theatre for him for a time.

Shura also knew and disliked the foreign men who came slumming it in the Badlands while pretending to lead upstanding lives in the Legation Quarter. He knew that Joe Knauf was vicious and evil, quick with his blade, a heroin dealer who adulterated his supplies with toxins. The excesses of these men brought trouble, they brought the police in, shining a spotlight on things best left in the shadows.

Yet war and revolution bring plagues on all houses, and Shura Giraldi's was no exception. Local legend had it that he escaped Peking after Pearl Harbor in a plane arranged by the Kuomintang (the ever useful Zaichek again?) and made it to Shanghai's French Concession, where he owned a high-class brothel full of fabulous treasure obtained from his burglaries. He saw out the war in comfort in Vichy-controlled, Japanese-protected Frenchtown, living as a woman, as the brothel's madam, and doubling his wealth despite paying exorbitant bribes to be left alone. After the war he and his treasure escaped to Hong Kong, said the rumours, this time by boat, avoiding armed Macanese pirates and British anti-smuggling patrols. There, in the British Crown colony, he dropped off the map into a well-earned obscurity.

A nice story, but untrue. If Shura ever did have significant wealth from stolen gems and banknotes, it was gone by 1945. He had lost his place at Paomachang, and the Badlands never recovered its former glory. Peking's foreign community, upright and underworld alike, had dwindled to only a handful. Hyper-inflation eroded any spending power they had left, the junkies died like flies as supplies dried up. Slowly the White Russian community, both the respectable and the less so, shrunk. Some went to the USSR, Russia being all they knew.

Most of the so-called 'Harbintsy' – who had been leaving voluntarily since 1937, and after 1945 in deportations as the Soviet Red Army occupied Harbin – disappeared into the gulags, inevitably accused of treachery and espionage by Stalin's paranoid regime. Others were luckier and were found new homes by the United Nations

Relief and Rehabilitation Administration or, slightly later, by the International Refugee Organisation, in the United States, Australia, Canada, Brazil, and elsewhere in South America. But it was often a horrific journey – many White Russians escaped civil-war-wracked China only to succumb in the disease-ridden refugee camp on Tubabao, and so never saw San Francisco, Sao Paulo or Melbourne.

For Shura, life after 1949 got even worse. The communists hounded him for his long-time affair with Zaichek – a close relationship with a senior Kuomintang official before the Japanese occupation was cause for persecution after Mao came to power. He appears to have been jailed for a time in the early 1950s, and this, as well as the rumours that continued to swirl around him regarding his criminal activities, meant he was not offered citizenship in any Western country.

But his friends stuck by him, his old boyfriends remained loyal, those of them still in China helping when they could. Sylvia, Tatiana Korovina's daughter, remembers Shura coming to the Tchoo family home for dinner and reminiscing with her mother and father about the heyday of the Badlands, its legendary characters and now shuttered venues. It was a case of troubles shared, troubles halved for what remained of the White Russian community in the chaos of postwar China.

Shura was among the last White Russians left stranded in the new People's Republic, one of a community whose numbers had dwindled to those few with absolutely nowhere to go. Eventually they were moved to Tientsin, to the once glorious but now rundown Talati Hotel on Victoria Road, to await their fate.

Shura was getting old, and tired, and he'd put on a little weight in later life. Gone the svelte, glamorous female figure, and the dapper man-about-town.

He was staying in a dilapidated room with hard iron beds and worn mattresses, though still with a young man for company. Some-one snapped his photograph there, showing the distinctive Siberian eyes – heavy-lidded, slightly sleepy, but penetrating even in a badly lit shot on an obviously cold day in a dismal room.

John Blofeld, who'd come to know Shura well in pre-war Peking, said of him that he had 'a nobility of character supported by an inner calm'. Even when penniless in Tientsin, during desperate times and facing an uncertain future, Shura does seem to have retained a certain calm nobility. He was perhaps the last denizen of the Bad-lands left in China, a true Peking decadent.

Repatriated to the Soviet Union in the late 1950s, to a Russia he had left more than forty years previously and now barely recognised, he is thought to have died there soon after arrival. And with his passing so finally passed the world he'd come to claim as his own; Shura Giraldi was to be the first and only King of Peking's Badlands.

Shura (left) and friend at the Talatai Hotel, 1950s

A Peking Badlands chorus line

Crossing the finish line at Paomachang

A Note on
Name Changes

Most place names have undergone some form of change in China since 1949, and a small note on those used in this text may be useful.

In Peking, which is now of course Beijing, Chuanpan Hutong is called Chuanban Hutong, Soochow Hutong is Suzhou Hutong, while Morrison Street – named after the Australian correspondent for *The Times* newspaper, George Morrison, better known as 'Morrison of Peking' – is now the thoroughfare of Wangfujing. The Grand Hôtel de Pékin still stands, but as the Grand Hotel Beijing, and is not far from what was Chienmen. The latter was redeveloped by Chairman Mao as Tiananmen Square.

Nearby, the former Dong'an Market still exists, in a considerably scaled-down form, as the Donghuamen Night Market. Very little now remains of Da Yuan Fu Hutong, which was adjacent to Morrison Street on its south-western side, and what is left is known as Datianshujing Hutong. The Hotel de la Paix is gone, having succumbed to redevelopment. The bustling thoroughfare of Hatamen Street, which separated the Badlands from the Legation Quarter, is now Chongwenmen Street. The former Legation Street, which ran through the heart of the Legation Quarter, is now Dong Jiangmi

Xiang. The old slum of Yang-I Hutong, home to so many Russian and European refugees in the 1930s, has long been bulldozed.

In Tientsin, now Tianjin, Bruce Road is called Yan Tai Dao. The old Racecourse Road has been split into Machang Dao and Zhejiang Road, while Victoria Road is Jiefang North Road – the hotel at number 158, which was the Talati Hotel, is now the First Business Hotel.

In Shanghai, the district of Hongkew, north of Suzhou Creek, is now Hongkou, while the Nanking Road is Nanjing West Road, and Kiangse Road is Jiangxi Road. The area known as the Hongkew Trenches was around Scott Road (now Shanyang Road), near Hongkew Park (now Lu Xun Park). It has long been completely redeveloped.

City names familiar to Westerners in the 1930s have changed too. Amoy is now Xiamen, Canton is Guangzhou, Chefoo is Yantai, Dairen is Dalian, Mukden is Shenyang, Newchwang is Yingkou, Port Arthur is Lushun, and Weihaiwei is Weihai. The Gulf of Pechili is now usually referred to as the Bohai Gulf. Manchuria is the province of Heilongjiang.

In Malaysia, Port Swettenham is now known as Port Klang.

Saigon is today called Ho Chi Minh City, where the Rue Catinat has become Dong Khoi.

Acknowledgements
and Sources

My thanks go primarily to Sylvia Walker, the daughter of Tatiana Korovina and Roy Tchoo, for sharing her memories of her remarkable parents and her childhood around the Badlands. Sadly, Sylvia passed away shortly after we began our correspondence in late 2011, but her husband Adrian was kind enough to continue the conversation with me. He also provided me with photos from Sylvia's family albums, those that survived the turmoil and chaos of war, revolution and relocation. As well as her own family's story, Sylvia told me the tale about Joe Knauf and other Badlands characters taking day trips to the Tien Chao execution grounds to see the killings there.

Sylvia also kindly contacted her network of old Peking White Russians for information on Shura. It flooded in. I know that many of the old China Hands who came out of that White Russian community didn't believe then, and many still don't believe now, that Shura Giraldi was involved in anything criminal whatsoever. But I'm afraid I have to beg to differ, as did the police of both Peking and Shanghai. The arguments around the true history and nature of Shura Giraldi will, I'm sure, continue as long as the old White Russian community of Peking is alive. The only indisputable fact is that Shura was a conundrum.

Many of the details used in these stories come from E.T.C. Werner's papers at the UK National Archives in Kew. Anyone wanting to consult them would be best advised to start at Document F3453/1510/10 (Far Eastern) and work from there. The years between autumn 1937 and the summer of 1940 that Werner spent trawling the dens and back streets of the Badlands in the hunt for the murderers of his daughter Pamela provide perhaps the best vignettes we have on record of the brief life and workings of the district.

Langdon Gilkey's memoir *Shantung Compound: The Story of Men and Women Under Pressure* (Harper & Row, New York, 1968) refers to the European dope addict rousted in the Badlands and sent to Weihsien Internment Camp as 'Briggs', which was a pseudonym, I believe. The ultimate resource for anyone wanting to track down the history of the internees is Greg Leck's exhaustive history, *Captives of Empire: The Japanese Internment of Allied Civilians in China (1941–1945),* (Shandy Press, Philadelphia, 2006).

The likely early backgrounds of Brana Shazker and Rosie Gerbert are typical of those outlined in Charles van Onselen's revealing and remarkable book *The Fox and the Flies: The World of Joseph Silver, Racketeer and Psychopath* (Jonathan Cape, London, 2007). Russian prostitutes such as Marie and Peggy, and madams such as Brana and Rosie, were nothing new in Peking and are referred to in many earlier memoirs, most notably that of the Tsarist diplomat Dmitrii Ivanovich Abrikosov, in *Revelations of a Russian Diplomat* (University of Washington Press, Seattle, 1964). Abrikosov recalls performing his diplomatic duties on behalf of Russia and escorting several Russian prostitutes and their madams to safety during the Boxer Rebellion of 1900.

To the best of my knowledge, Marie and Peggy are only recorded in E.T.C. Werner's archive at Kew. The well-known and much-liked Father Paul Shelaeff talked about his years as a Russian Orthodox priest in Harbin during a number of interviews he gave to the California press after his son Andre died. Andre, a gifted boxer who became Welterweight Champion of the Orient, was destined for greater things in America, but he died of a cerebral haemorrhage shortly after a fight in San Francisco's National Hall in December 1938.

Joe Knauf, too, lives on largely in the descriptions of him left by Werner in his archives, though there are also references to him in the documents left by Arthur Ringwalt, the highly respected Third Secretary at the American Legation in Peking in the late 1930s. During the course of monitoring undesirable and problematic Americans in northern China, Ringwalt opened a file on Knauf as a possible collaborator, and noted Michael Consiglio as another American involved in criminal activities in the Badlands. Several people who grew up in the Badlands, among them Sylvia Walker, remember their parents specifically warning them to keep away from Knauf, such was his notoriety.

For the most detailed descriptions of the Kavkaz bar and Shura as a 'wine merchant' in the 1930s, see John Blofeld's *City of Lingering Splendour: A Frank Account of Old Peking's Exotic Pleasures* (Hutchinson, London, 1961), which includes occasional mentions of other White Russians and foreigners who delved into the Badlands, or who sojourned in Peking between the wars. It is also worth mentioning Julia Boyd's recently published *A Dance With the Dragon: The Vanished World of Peking's Foreign Colony* (I.B. Tauris, London, 2012). And when it comes to those Western bohemians who occasionally enjoyed a night's slumming in Peking, Harold Acton's *Peonies and Ponies* (Chatto & Windus, London, 1941) is a must-read for an evocation of the extreme loucheness and grand bitchiness of the era.

IMAGE CREDITS

Pages 19, 20 & 64, all pictures of Tatiana Korovina and Roy Tchoo in Peking, as well as Shura Giraldi in Tientsin, courtesy of Sylvia and Adrian Walker; pages 28 & 46, Hong Kong's Lyndhurst Terrace and The Grand Hôtel de Pékin, from author's collection; pages 28 & 34, advert for Whisker's Girl House and Japanese troops entering Peking in August 1937, courtesy of Getty Images; pages 34 & 46, picture of Japanese troops patrolling Peking street and Hatamen Street, courtesy of Corbis; page 46, Peking advertising billboards, courtesy of the Fred Jewell Collection and John Cornelius; page 64, image of horse racing at Paomachang, courtesy of the Michael Hanley Lawless Collection and www.chinamarine.org, Peking chorus line girls, courtesy of Graham Earnshaw.

Read on for an excerpt of
Paul French's

MIDNIGHT IN PEKING

How the murder of a young Englishwoman haunted the last days of old China

The eastern section of old Peking has been dominated since the fifteenth century by a massive watchtower, built as part of the Tartar Wall to protect the city from invaders. Known as the Fox Tower, it was believed to be haunted by fox spirits, a superstition that meant the place was deserted at night.

After dark the area became the preserve of thousands of bats, which lived in the eaves of the Fox Tower and flitted across the moonlight like giant shadows. The only other living presence was the wild dogs, whose howling kept the locals awake. On winter mornings the wind stung exposed hands and eyes, carrying dust from the nearby Gobi Desert. Few people ventured out early at this time of year, opting instead for the warmth of their beds.

But just before dawn on 8 January 1937, rickshaw pullers passing along the top of the Tartar Wall, which was wide enough to walk or cycle on, noticed lantern lights near the base of the Fox Tower, and indistinct figures moving about. With neither the time nor the inclination to stop, they went about their business, heads down, one foot in front of the other, avoiding the fox spirits that were out seeking victims.

When daylight broke on another freezing day, the tower was deserted once more. The colony of bats circled one last time before the creeping sun sent them back to their eaves. But in the wasteland between the road and the tower, the wild dogs – the huang gou, or yellow dogs – were circling curiously, sniffing at something alongside a ditch. It was the body of a young woman, lying at an odd angle and covered by a layer of frost. Her clothing was dishevelled, her body badly mutilated. On her wrist was an expensive watch that had stopped just after midnight.

It was the morning after the Russian Christmas, which was thirteen days after the Western Christmas by the old Julian calendar, and the corpse belonged to nineteen-year-old Pamela Werner, an Englishwoman who'd been born and raised in Peking. When news of her murder broke it sent waves of fear through the city's already nervous foreign community.

New York Times Bestseller

Coming to TV Soon
Over 100000 copies sold worldwide
12 foreign language editions

For more information visit:
www.penguin.com.au/authors/paul-french

Follow the Mysteries . . .

Also by Paul French

 www.chinarhyming.com

 @chinarhyming

 @oldshanghaipaul

 paul@chinarhyming.com